**THE LAZY WAY TO E[N]**
**AND**
**UNLIMITED H[A]**

## Freddy H. Jacquin

'Art is a lie that that makes us realise the truth.'
Pablo Picasso

This book is dedicated to the memory of my mother Sylvia, who more than anyone else, shaped my thinking and belief in myself, and whose love for me, never faltered.

Thank you to everyone who has ever encouraged me to pursue my dreams, fearlessly.

To everyone who has shown me love.

To everyone who has believed in me and those who still believe.

Thanks also to all those who without knowing have contributed to this book, with their knowledge, understanding and love.

Special thanks to my friend Felicia J Ursarescu, who designed the book cover, and allowed me to use her original artwork for the cover and the pictures throughout this book.

Also, to Clara Benali for her editing skills.

THE LAZY WAY TO ENLIGHTENMENT AND
UNLIMITED HAPPINESS
First published 2020. © Freddy Jacquin.

*This work is owned and published by Freddy Jacquin.*

*The right of Freddy Jacquin to be identified as the author of this work has been asserted by him in accordance with the UK Copyright, Designs and Patents Act 1988. All rights reserved worldwide.*

*No part of this publication may be stored in retrieval system, transmitted or reproduced or shared in any way, including but not limited to digital copying and printing, without the prior agreement and written permission of the author. You must not use our products for commercial use, except for the purposes of your own personal development. You may not copy or make copies of these products and give them to others, without the expressed written, dated and signed permission of the author.*

About the author, Freddy H Jacquin, B.Sc.

Freddy H Jacquin is the founder and principal of the UK Hypnotherapy Training College (Jacquin Hypnosis Academy) which he created in 1999.

Over the past 28 years he has been influential in changing the perception of hypnotherapy and the use of trance as a therapeutic tool for positive change.

The contents of this book are based on the techniques he has learned and developed, and the experience gained from dealing with thousands of clients with a multitude of various problems.

He has personally developed techniques that enable him to move people rapidly to a resolution of their problems.

He has worked with more than 35,000 clients to help them achieve freedom from self-imposed limitations, physical and emotional pain and negative programming by others.

THE LAZY WAY TO ENLIGHTENMENT AND
UNLIMITED HAPPINESS

*This book has the potential to change your life, but for that to happen you must realise that this is a collaboration between you and the author, and designed for you to take an active role in the process.*
*Enjoy!*

Between illusion and reality lays the truth.

## Contents

| Page: | |
|---|---|
| 10 | *Chapter 1: Learning and habitual behaviour* |
| 19 | *Chapter 2: Pleasure and pain* |
| 22 | *Chapter 3: Clearing the ground: Eliminating limiting beliefs, irrational doubts and fears* |
| 33 | *Chapter 4: Building strong foundations: Increasing self-belief, self-esteem and self-confidence* |
| 40 | *Chapter 5: Finding your 'Self'* |
| 45 | *Chapter 6: Unlimited Happiness* |
| 49 | *Chapter 7: Physical and emotional pain control* |
| 54 | *Chapter 8: Accessing Neutral* |
| 58 | *Chapter 9: Total perception management, for accessing neutral emotion* |
| 64 | *Chapter 10: TPM to increase a positive emotional state* |
| 69 | *Chapter 11: Need, want, desire: Manifesting your dreams.* |
| 75 | *Chapter12: Enlightenment and unlimited happiness: Putting it all together* |

Whether we want to acknowledge it or not, our lives are governed by desires and fear. Our brain has evolved, but its basic purpose has remained the same. Humankind (homo sapiens) have evolved as a species but our basic needs remain the same.

These needs could be described as the need for pleasure and protection. As with all animals, these basic needs originated as survival and procreation.

We may have evolved as a species because of civilisation, social structures, social rules and constraints, but the basic needs for protection and pleasure (survival and procreation) remain the driving force of our behaviour.

Most, if not all psychological problems, derive from continually attempting and mostly failing to suppress, ignore, hide or feel guilty about these psychological and physical drivers.

In other words we spend our lives fighting our true nature. This of course is necessary in a civilised society, but this suppression is the main cause of psychological problems, physical and mental illness. Let us for a moment look at the two main, self-inflicted causes of premature death, smoking cigarettes and obesity.

1.3 billion people smoke cigarettes; do these people smoke for pleasure?

If you ask someone who smokes cigarettes why they do it, rarely if ever will their first answer be, 'enjoyment'. The answer will be something to do with relaxation or calm.

For those who have been convinced that they are addicted to nicotine, then another reason is to avoid the pain of withdrawal from the drug.

At the time of writing this (2020), for the first time in the history of mankind, the number of people dying from obesity has overtaken the number of people who are dying from starvation.

So, the question is, 'Why do people continue to kill themselves with food, alcohol and drugs'?

If it is not for pleasure, then it is for perceived protection.
So, what has this do with enlightenment and happiness?

This book has been written and is designed to give

you, the reader, complete control of your life: spiritual, emotional, physical and psychological.

The majority, of people believe or feel that so many aspects of their life are out of their control.

Social laws, physical, psychological and financial limitations, even our own cultural and religious beliefs and those of others, that are imposed upon us, contribute to this belief.

How can we possibly be truly happy or fulfilled with so many constraints?

This book is designed to show you how.

## Chapter 1
## Learning and habitual behaviour

As human beings we have an incredible ability to learn complex patterns of behaviour or skills.

We are able, to learn incredibly complex things to the point that we can carry the behaviour out without any conscious awareness or thought.

Driving a car is probably the most obvious example.

When we first attempt to learn to drive a car there seems to be a hundred things to think about at the same time.

Then, over a period of time we learn to drive safely, and we receive a licence to drive. At some point after that, we find ourselves driving safely, making thousands of adjustments on the steering wheel, working the pedals and gears, without having to consciously think about what we are doing.

Along with the ability to learn something as complex as driving a car and then allowing it to become an unconscious ability or skill, there are hundreds, maybe even thousands of abilities and skills that we can now carry out without thinking. Speaking, reading, walking, riding a bicycle, typing or playing a musical instrument are just a few examples. This natural ability enables us to function at the level that we function as human beings.

If you can read English, it is impossible to look at these words and not read them, yet there was a time when reading was impossible for you to do. Now reading is an automatic function, something you can do without thinking.

Unfortunately, where this works against us is when we learn something, or are taught something, or are told something that is not true or that turns out to be detrimental to us.

Smoking cigarettes is probably the best example. No one starts smoking 20 cigarettes a day and inhaling the smoke from their very first cigarette. It takes time and effort to train the lungs and brain to accept the smoke and chemicals.
Over time, the body learns to accept the 3000+ chemicals, but it takes time to do so.

In that period of time the same thing occurs that occurs with everything that we learn, and eventually smoking cigarettes becomes an unconscious automatic function, and as with walking, reading and driving a car, it is almost if not absolutely impossible to change consciously.

It has been said that more than 60% of our beliefs about who we are, what we believe is right or wrong, what we believe we can or cannot achieve, and even who we believe we are, was created and decided upon by a child of under seven years old.

The same goes for most of our irrational fears and doubts.

This is a scary thought, as I doubt that you would have a child of three or four years old making a life-long decision about what you are capable of, or what is true or false.

By the time we reach adulthood our mind has created a defence mechanism known as the critical faculty.

I like to think of this as a tightly knitted mesh, a filter over our brain that protects us against lies, flattery, sales techniques and false beliefs.

As a child this defence mechanism has not yet formed, therefore the child will believe almost anything he or she is told. As a child we believe (if we have been told so) that Santa is an actual person and that fairy tales are true. This is of course true for religious beliefs.

The religious beliefs that someone is willing to fight for and even die for, are totally dependent on what parents they are born to, or what country or culture they are born in.

The same thing occurs when as a child we are in the presence of someone who is afraid: we pick up on the emotion and tend to take on the fear or phobia ourselves.

No one is born with a fear of snakes, spiders, wasps, sharp objects, heights or water.

Most if not all irrational fears are learned from someone rather than experienced personally, as are most, if not all, of our limiting beliefs and negative thoughts about ourselves.

If we are afraid of an object, creature, person or persons but have never actually experienced physical or emotional pain from the object, creature, person or persons, then all the fear, the perceived threat, exists only in our imagination.

As an example, let us look at a common phobia,

spiders!

If you live in the UK as I do, there are no spiders that can harm you, yet many people in the UK are petrified of spiders; why is this?

If as a child, you see a parent or an adult displaying fear when they see a spider, you imagine that there must be something about spiders that is dangerous, (*of course in some countries this can be true, granted*) but the child has never at this point been hurt by a spider. The child now imagines what it would be like to be hurt by a spider, and feels afraid, then their body reacts as if it is true.

This imagination over time becomes automatic, eventually the child forgets that they are only imagining the danger, and as with all imagination, when we forget that we are only imagining, to the body and mind it is real. The child sees a spider and the brain floods the body with adrenaline in preparation to run or fight.

Once the above paragraph is understood, you may want to think about all of the irrational fears and beliefs you have; and knowing it has only ever been just your imagination and not reality, decide to stop imagining it. What? I hear you cry, 'just stop imagining it?' Yes, just stop imagining it or imagine it differently because either way it is not real.

Just for a moment think about what you have just read, because this book will show you how to undermine and eliminate all of your irrational fears, and perceived limitations.

There are two ways to develop a phobic response or a limiting belief.

Every piece of information that comes in through our senses, Kinaesthetic (touch), Olfactory (smell), Auditory (sound) and taste (Gustatory), passes through the part of the brain known as the Amygdala.

The Amygdala is probably the most primitive part of a human being and every animal with a vertebra, has an Amygdala.

We can think of the Amygdala as the gate keeper: Throughout our life the Amygdala is storing information on pleasure and pain and it works with all our sensory modalities.

If a dog bites you, the instant that you feel the pain, the Amygdala is storing every piece of information related to the pain, what the animal looks like, smells like and sounds like.

This information will be downloaded and stored as a template in a millisecond. Then for the rest of your life the Amygdala will be scanning the environment for anything that looks, smells or sounds like a dog, and will automatically prepare your body to run or fight by flooding your body with adrenalin. This is known as the flight or fight response.

This instant learning can occur with physical and emotional pain.

If someone hurts you emotionally, the instant that you feel the pain, everything about that person, the way they look, smell and sound will (in the same way as described above in the dog example) be stored and a template will be created.

If this occurs when we are very young, we may consciously forget about the experience, but the Amygdala never forgets. This could explain why sometimes we meet someone who appears to be nice, but all of our senses are telling us to be cautious of that person.

This of course happens with pleasurable emotional experiences as well. If you experience pleasure with someone, the Amygdala will store all the sensual information relating to that experience, in the same way as it does a strong negative experience. Your first, really strong, positive sexual experience and all the sensual information attached to the experience will be stored and any of the elements of that pleasurable experience will always excite you.

There are two sets of nerves that run through our extremities to our brain.

Both pass through the Amygdala, the first set of nerves are wired to the area of the brain that reasons and makes decisions.

The second set though, is wired directly to the Amygdala at which point the Amygdala acts independently.

If you had five objects in your pocket and you put your hand into your pocket, you could determine which each object was without seeing it. This is the function of the first set of nerves.

However, if one of the objects in your pocket was sharp and you pricked your finger, the Amygdala would make an executive decision instantly and you would, without having to think about it, pull your hand immediately out of your pocket.

We do not have to get burned five times by an object before we realise that touching that object hurts.

The instant that you touch that object and you feel the pain, the Amygdala fires up and stores the information and then for the rest of your life, it is scanning the environment for anything that looks like that object, so that you don't get hurt again.

This book will show you how to use this incredible albeit primitive part of our brain to change your life, your physical, emotional, psychological and spiritual self, and achieve the life that you truly want.

## Chapter 2
## Pleasure and pain

We often hear people speaking about the mind, expressions such as 'If I just put my mind on it', 'You must have the right mindset', ' She is strong minded', 'He has a filthy mind', It's all in your mind'.

If you were to ask a brain surgeon if she has a mind, she will probably say 'yes'. If you ask someone where their mind is, they will probably tap their head. We often hear psychologists and psychiatrists speaking about the conscious and the unconscious or subconscious mind.

Here though is the thing, no one has ever seen a mind or held one in their hand.
The wonderful thing about the mind is that it only exists as a concept created by our imagination and imagination is created by (you guessed it) the mind.

The German language does not have an equivalent word for the mind. Does this mean that the millions of people who speak German do not have a mind? It is more likely to be the case that no one has a mind.

'I think, therefore I am'. This is a famous, well

known quote.

Do *you* really, 'think', though? Do you know, what you were thinking this time yesterday, or what you will be thinking three thoughts from now?

'I think therefore I am', or should it be 'I am therefore I think'. What if it is, that you actually have no control of what you are thinking, but you only have control of what thoughts you act upon or not act upon?

Let us for a moment think about what is known as a Human-being.

The human-being or more precisely the organism known as a human, consists of a body and a brain. Each have many component parts of which this book is too limited in size to detail, and that depth of information is not why you purchased this book.

Beyond the body and the brain, mankind has endowed the human being with intangible aspects, a soul, a spirit and of course a mind. None of these aspects of a human has ever been seen, felt, heard, smelt or for that matter photographed.

If you think this sounds depressing or that I am just

negating how wonderful the human is, I can reassure you that I love every aspect of being human, I accept and celebrate every emotion that makes us human, love, passion, pleasure, joy and even pain.

I do though have complete control over all the above mentioned, emotions, and this book is written to enable you to do the same.

My intention in writing this book is to enable you to enjoy your life, every aspect of it to the full.

## Chapter 3
## Clearing the ground: Eliminating, limiting beliefs, irrational doubts and fears

Think of this book as a blueprint for your perfect life. If it were a blueprint for your perfect house, then we are looking at a plot of land, to build that house on.

The first thing we need to do is clear the ground, eliminate any rocks and boulders, tree stumps and rubbish.

We then need to put in strong foundations to build your house upon, and all the services that will keep your house running.

Then we will start building your dream house; for this to happen, you have to have a clear plan and a blueprint of exactly what you want your house to be.

Once the structure of the house is up and it is weathered to keep out the elements, you can then start to do the interior design. Things that bring you comfort and joy.

So, we will start by clearing the plot, eliminating any limiting beliefs, negative thoughts and irrational fears and doubts from your life.

As I stated in chapter one, the ability to learn something to the point where it becomes an ability or skill, something we can do, without conscious thought being involved, enables us as human beings to function at the level that we function.

The downside to this ability, to learn something to this level of functioning, is that at that point we no longer have conscious control over the action or behaviour.

This same structure of learning as described in chapter two, is how we develop a natural defence, a natural concern and unfortunately, also an irrational fear or phobia.

At the point that the learning becomes an automatic function, behaviour, fear, ability or an unconscious action, it is as if we create a part of us that then runs the action automatically.

How often have you wanted to be free of a detrimental behaviour or habit and said, 'I would love to be free, but there is part of me that just won't let me'.
Although there is a part of you that now knows that none of these thoughts exist outside of your head,

except as perception, we still use this form of language to express our limitations, and it is closer to the truth than you may know.

You have a part of you that can drive a car, a part that can ride a bicycle, a part that can read, a part that can write and perhaps a hundred parts of your being that run other programs that enable you to be the incredible person that you are.

This book will enable you to look at each individual psychological part/program and re-assess its function or purpose and decide whether the program is still of use or is now redundant or detrimental.

Then having made the decision from a completely neutral emotional state, you can communicate at an unconscious level with the part responsible for the unwanted behaviour, fear or habitual program and decide whether to allow the program to continue to run or change the program at a molecular, cellular, neuronal level, so that it functions in a positive way that serves your highest intention.

Firstly though, you need to create the blueprint of your dream life.

Start by clearing the ground: Take the time now if

you can, let go of any perceived limitations and on the next two pages of this book write down the things you want to be free of; irrational fears, doubts, limiting beliefs, negative thoughts about your abilities or self-worth.

Start building your dream life: Write down your goals, physical, financial, emotional and spiritual. You will see there is a lot of space to do so, so let your mind run without limitations.

The next section of this book is also available as an audio session in which I will personally guide you into an inner focus of attention, where you will have access to the part of you that runs the redundant or unwanted, unconscious behaviours and habitual programming.

You will then negotiate and create an updated program which will enable you to have the life you desire.

You can access and download the audio session from this link.

https://freddyjacquin.com/partsnegotiation

Clearing the ground: Eliminating irrational fear, anxiety, stress and panic and negative habitual behaviour.

When you are ready to liberate yourself from fear and anxiety and every perceived limitation, find a place where you can read this section or listen to the audio session, undisturbed.

Now you are ready to make these first changes on your journey to enlightenment and unlimited happiness and freedom.

As you read these words, focus on your breathing and as you become aware of your breathing, start to breath deeper with each breath and allow your body to begin to relax.

Now as you continue reading, notice that your body is relaxing automatically, and your mind is becoming less and less aware of the environment and the sounds around you.

You may become aware of the comfort of the chair, the sound of your breathing, the beating of your heart, certain sensations and the thoughts that drift in and out of your mind, automatically.

Just for a moment think about the people that you love, the people that love you. See those faces and feel that love, see those smiles and notice as you feel that love that every negative thought and limiting belief is dropping away from you.

Because as you continue to read and breathe deeper you become less and less aware of your physical body, exactly where the hands or the fingers are positioned, even the effort it takes to be aware of which leg is relaxing more than the other becomes to much effort to bother making.

The mind drifting down toward a place of peace and calm as you continue to read these words and each word now relaxes you more and more.

Imagine now that this is happening automatically and there is nothing you can do about it.

The more you read the calmer you become.

Now as the calm, inner quiet grows, you can use your unconscious mind as a resource that you can learn from and really have a unique experience, now.

Imagine now that the part of you that is running and is responsible for the habit, fear or behaviour that you would like to change, is forming in front of you.

In your own mind, silently just ask that part of you what its purpose is, what it has been trying to do for you. Wait for the answer, which will come.

Now you know the reason for doing what it is you want to change, thank that part for doing it.

Now ask the part to go to your creative mind and allow that creative part of you to run, flow and work and come up with some new choices, better ways to satisfy the positive intention of that part of you.

New choices and behaviours that will keep you safe and well but also allow you the freedom that you want.

Assume that this is happening now as you continue to read, totally unaware of your physical being but aware of certain changes taking place in your mind as you continue to read these words.

You will find yourself drifting as a mind, back to the very first moment that relates to the problem, but you are drifting back with all the understanding that you have now as an adult, with all the strength you have now. Be brave, this is the last time this will ever affect you in a negative way.

You remember where you were, remember now the event, see that younger you just about to go through the experience. Drop down beside that younger you, reassure that younger you that you survived the experience. Say what is needed to be said, that will allow that younger self be the best adult they can be.

Store the strength and learnings in that part of your mind that is there for such learnings and now when you are ready to free yourself forever, give that younger you a hug and say goodbye.

Step over the line into your future and turn around and see that younger you, with a smile on their face waving goodbye as you free them forever. Now close the door behind you.

Now once again focus on the part of you that runs the behaviour and ask it to choose one of the new choices.

Now ask it to integrate those new changes into your body and your mind, now.

As you now become aware of those changes in your mind and body, close your eyes for five seconds, now.

Notice the changes that you are feeling now and I don't know whether it will be minutes from now, an hour from now or twenty years from now, when you suddenly realise that you have been thinking of something else entirely and every irrational fear has gone.

Use this section as often as you need to, on all your doubts and fears until you are totally aware that you are completely free.

## Chapter 4
## Building strong foundations: Increasing self-belief, self-esteem and self-confidence

We are born believing that we can do anything and with an innate intelligence.

If you were to hold a handful of flowers seeds in your hand, chances are that it would be impossible for you to discern the rose seed from the marigold or the daisy, (unless of course you are an expert on growing flowers). Yet within each seed there is a blueprint of what it has the potential to become.

All any seed needs is the correct environment and nourishment, to achieve its potential.

Within each child, in the moment of conception, the same natural intelligence exists.

Then the child is born and as with the flower seed, all it needs is the correct, safe environment and nourishment to achieve its potential.

For the human-being to thrive, the nourishment needed is more than just food, water and a safe environment.

We have a need for physical touch and affection.

In the United States, in the 1940s an experiment was conducted on newly born infants to determine whether individuals could thrive alone on basic physiological needs without affection.

Twenty newly born infants were housed in a facility where they were fed, bathed and their diapers changed. The caregivers had been instructed not to look at or touch the babies more than was necessary, never communicating with them.

All the child's physical needs were attended to scrupulously and the environment was kept sterile, none of the babies became ill. The experiment was halted after four months, by which time, at least half of the babies had died.

At least two more died even after being rescued and brought into a more natural familial environment.

There was no physiological cause for the babies deaths; they were all physically very healthy.
The conclusion was that nurturing is a very vital need in humans.

Whilst this was taking place, in a separate facility,

the second group of twenty newly born infants were raised with all their basic physiological needs provided and the addition of affection from the caregivers. This time however, the outcome was as expected, with no deaths encountered.

We need purpose and we also need to feel a part of something greater than ourselves.

Without a purpose or the feeling that we are part of something bigger than ourselves, and touch and affection, we can survive but we cannot thrive.

When we are born, we are unaware of any limitations, everything seems possible. As we grow, we soon learn what our physical limitations are, and these of course differ from one person to another.

We also learn our mental capabilities and limitations, but unlike the physical limitations we have, many of our mental limitations are placed on us, or suggested to us, as are many if not all, of our beliefs.

As this is the case, this means that the majority of our mental and emotional limitations and beliefs, including religious ones, turn out to be no more than someone else's opinion.

Once this is understood, we can begin to choose what we want to believe, on the simple basis of, 'does this belief empower me or disempower me?'

The next question then is, 'how badly do I want to feel, behave or live differently?'

What if changing your life, emotional state and negative habitual behaviours was as easy as just changing your mind and then being fearless enough to do what suits you?

Of course, no man is an island as the saying goes and very often by the time we come to the realisation that we are not fulfilled, happy or satisfied with our life any longer, we are already in the matrix known as 'life', family, children, shared finances, social constraints and 'responsibilities'.

You the reader are obviously not completely fulfilled or happy otherwise you would not be reading this book.

Here then is the question, 'What do you want?'

The answer to that question will have immediately appeared to you, even though you may have instantly dismissed it; you may have even pushed the thought out of your mind.

You may be feeling guilty for even thinking it, because the answer to what it is that would allow you to be completely happy, may go against your moral or religious beliefs, or what you deem to be acceptable, responsible behaviour.

We spoke earlier about the need to feel part of something bigger than ourselves. If we are lucky, we have family, friends and colleagues, our tribe if you like.

As with any tribe there are rules, even laws that if you do not adhere to, could lead to you being ostracised or even punished.

The need to be accepted is also a basic need. We feel safer within a group and stepping out or away from our tribe, even though we may know that our ultimate happiness and fulfilment is dependent on doing so, is not an easy thing to do.

To maintain any semblance of 'self' is difficult to do when surrounded by or embroiled in this matrix we call 'life'.

So, many people search for this awareness of 'self'

through meditation, therapy, religion and in altered states created by drugs, alcohol or sex.

All of the above can enable us to have a glimpse of the 'Self', but it is generally fleeting.

A fleeting glimpse is enough though, to know that we want to maintain the feeling and the ability that it gives us.

So, we continue the search, unfulfilled at a fundamental level.

This inner dissatisfaction is felt in us as a need, although we may be unaware of what it is that we need.

For many it is mistaken as hunger, hence the worldwide obesity problem. Others try to fulfil the need with alcohol, drugs, sex, gambling, pornography or even the gym.

My belief is that anyone who is doing anything to excess, is unconsciously trying to fill this unconscious awareness of a need.

In the next chapter we will discuss this in detail, and I will attempt to show you how to be fulfilled on every level.

## Chapter 5
## Finding your 'self'

The search for 'self' and the meaning of life. 'Who am I'? 'Why am I here'? 'What is my purpose'?

These questions have been asked throughout the ages. Many religious scholars, philosophers, mystics, pilgrims and other individuals have tried and failed to find the answer to these questions.

How to separate the 'I' from the 'I am' or the 'me' is what you will discover in this book and once you understand that you are not your name, body or thoughts, this awareness will set you free.

The essence of who you are is an intangible part of the organism that you call 'You'. Some, depending on their religious beliefs, may call this 'Essence', the spirit or the soul.

What I mean by the 'Essence' is the observer, the passenger, the part of you that observes you behaving badly or cruelly, or kindly and lovingly.

You are not your body, because you could lose an arm and still be you, you could lose a leg and still be you. What part of your physical being would have to be removed for 'you' to no longer exist?

The essence of 'You' is just a passenger housed within the organism that you call 'Your body'.

The essence of who you are though, cannot move, communicate or experience life as we know it without the physical body.

Once this is understood, you will begin to care more about this physical vehicle that enables you to experience life, pleasure and pain.

The human physical organism is less than 2% different to that of a chimpanzee. The two percent difference may well be the 'Essence' or the 'Self', the highest intelligence in the known universe.

Unfortunately, this highest of all known intelligences, is housed in a chimp.

Chimpanzees are closely related to the great apes and if you were to observe a great ape in its natural habitat you would see that all a great ape wants to do is sit, eat and whenever possible mate.

The essence of who you are wants to learn, to love, to feel, to enjoy and connect with other human beings at the 'Essence' level.

The essence of who you are wants to experience life at a higher level, to discover, create, develop, invent and experience emotions beyond the animal level of survival and procreation.

To do this we have to tame the animal we are housed in, that we co-habit with.

This balance is where peace is found. We have to let the animal live, have fun, have a certain amount of freedom, feed it properly, care for it, even love it.

If we, because of social restraints, religious beliefs or social rules, deny the animal its basic needs or continually restrain it, it will, as all animals do when chained up or caged, get angry, sad and ill.

This fine balancing act begins with this understanding.

When we continually deny ourselves and repress our needs, we will become obsessed with that which we are repressing.

*The other side of the coin of repression is obsession.*

We do not need to lock ourselves up in a monastery or walk barefoot for a thousand miles to discover our self, because the self is within us. We just need to be.

Most of our communication with others is at the 'I am' level: I am Freddy, I am a father, I am a writer.

Sometimes we communicate at the 'me or my' level, this is my house, this is my body, this is my job, this is my family.

Sometimes we communicate at the animal level, sexual desire, smell, physical attraction.

Rarely do we meet someone that we can communicate with at the 'Essence' level, more commonly known as spiritual level. We sometimes hear people say, 'I have found my soul mate'.

When this occurs, it is a rare and beautiful thing. This is because the 'Essence' has no physical boundaries, it is timeless, it does not exist within the constraints of the imagination of mere mortals, it is infinite.

To access the 'Self', the 'Essence' of who you are, find a place where you can be completely undisturbed and return to the neutral state that you have learned, or will learn, how to do in chapter eight, or from the audio session that accompanies that chapter; then just be, with the intention of accessing the 'Self'.

Once you have achieved this, you will realise that nothing that happens to your physical being can touch you, not even death.

You will take the observer position of your physical being, so if the body is suffering pain, you can say, 'that's interesting, my body is suffering, but it cannot affect me', and then observe rather than be involved.

The Audio for this section of the book in chapter eight will enable you to access a neutral state and therefore access the 'Essence' of you.

## Chapter 6
## Unlimited Happiness

What is unlimited happiness? Does such a thing exist and if so, is it possible to achieve it?

Once again it is time to ask your 'self' a question, 'What is it that you believe will allow you to be or make you happy?'

Have you ever observed a child or maybe a pet of yours having fun and felt happy just watching them?

Now you can take the observer position and enjoy your life with the same pleasure. Even your mistakes can be observed with the same pleasure that we derive from watching a child learning to walk or speak.

Someone once told me that we are gods in training; from that viewpoint we can forgive ourselves for the mistakes that we make because we are not the finished item, YET!

Many of us, and that probably includes you, have at some point said, 'I will be happy when…' I'll be happy when I have more money, find the right partner, pay off my mortgage, lose weight or a hundred other utterances. Michael Neals in his book, 'How to be happy now', states that if you are doing things in order to be happy, you are doing things in the wrong order.

The answer is to find the things in your life that you can be happy about right now, no matter how small.

Take that time now before you read on, think of something that you can be happy about in this moment.

This will not stop you from striving to have the things you desire or achieving your dreams, but because you are happy now, your happiness no longer depends on you getting those things.

From this solid platform of happiness, you will find that not only will you achieve your goals and desires, you will do so faster and with a smile on your face.

You may be reading this book because you are terminally ill and are looking for answers for the meaning of your existence. Maybe you are wondering, how can you be happy when you are suffering or in pain.

I would ask you once again to re-read the previous

chapter and although it may take some practice, separate your 'self' from your physical being.

Very few of us want to die, and it is natural when we are ill to ask, 'why me?' The real question though is, 'why not me'?

As I have stated I am not a religious person and I don't personally believe in a heaven and a hell, except for those that we create here on Earth, but I do believe that as the essence of who we are is intangible, it cannot be destroyed.

The organism our essence is housed in or inhabits will breakdown, disintegrate and 'die', that is inevitable; but what if when that occurs it just frees the 'essence' to find another host to continue the god training? True or not it is a great thought.

Find the happiness in this moment no matter how much pain the physical body is in, just observe with curiosity and wonder. Once this occurs you can separate yourself completely from the pain your body is in.

Remember though that if you are experiencing physical pain, it is initially a warning and must be deemed chronic, unnecessary pain by a medical practitioner before you eliminate it.

The next chapter will help you do that, whether the pain is physical or emotional.

Alternatively, you can listen to the audio session that you can download here.
https://freddyjacquin.com/paincontrol

## Chapter 7
## Physical and emotional pain control

As you read these words, do your utmost to imagine what I am describing, in whatever way comes to mind.

Firstly, for a moment focus on the pain that you are experiencing and on a score of 0-10, ten being excruciating and zero being no pain at all, say that number to yourself.

Because in a while from now, you will be unable to feel the pain.

Now sit as comfortably as you can, and as you read these words let your imagination run.

Take a deep breath in and as you exhale start to feel your body relaxing, more and more with each breath.

Imagine as you do this, that you are beginning to drift up out of your body and leaving your body in the chair.

You may even be able to see yourself sitting in the chair reading these words as you drift higher and further away from your body.

Imagine that you are drifting higher and higher, like a helium balloon that a young child has let go of in the park, drifting higher and higher, further and further away from your body in that chair.

Imagine now that you have drifted so high that you can look down and see the planet Earth below you, you can see that beautiful blue planet in your mind's eye.

You can see the whites of the mountain tops, the white of the clouds, the green of the forest and the blue of the ocean.

Notice as you watch that beautiful planet from so far away, how your perspective changes.

You can think about the 7 billion people living on that planet of which you are one, notice as you think about that, how things that had seemed overwhelming, no longer have any power over you, things that had seemed difficult, even impossible, no longer have any power over you.

Now in your mind's eye picture a target, like an archery target way down below you between you and that beautiful blue planet, a massive target, you can see the coloured bands and you can see the very centre of that target.

In the centre of the target is every ounce of the chronic, useless, unnecessary pain, both physical and emotional that you were experiencing.

In a moment you will read a specific word, an instruction, and as you read that word you will feel yourself propelled through space in your mind, like an arrow. You will feel yourself fly right through the centre of the target in a millisecond, and out the other side into a space of bliss, but I want you to be brave because as you fly through the centre of the target you may experience the pain even more intensely for a split second; but be brave, this is the last time it will ever affect you. So, get ready for the word.

*NOW*

And now you are through the target and out the other side just floating in a space of bliss. Think of the people you love, people that love you, and feel that love now, like a burning hot sun in a summer sky. Shrink that down to a burning hot nuclear powered ball of light, as big as a golf ball, and pull that light and love into the very core of your being, into the very centre of your being. Feel the force of that love and light flooding your body and your mind, spreading into every cell, every molecule, into the very marrow of your bones. Lighting you up lifting you up, now.

Now imagine drifting across the other side of your room so that you can see yourself sitting in that chair reading. You can see the clothes that you are wearing and notice, as you watch yourself reading from the other side of the room, how every ounce of the useless unnecessary pain that you were experiencing has gone from your mind and your body. You cannot feel it, you cannot experience it.

The harder you try and remember what it felt like, the further from you mind it goes.

Now as you read this, your mind will allow you to drift back over to your body in that chair and drop down and reintegrate back into your body, unable to feel any of the discomfort or pain. Go ahead take your time.

Where has the pain gone now? Try to feel it and find that you cannot. On a scale of one to ten 'Where has the pain GONE now? It will never affect you again. Enjoy!

## Chapter 8
## Accessing Neutral

Now you have eliminated all your irrational fears and limiting beliefs and changed any negative habitual behaviours that were holding you back.

Now you realise that the essence of who you truly are cannot be touched by any physical changes in your body, and that because nothing actually exists outside of your skull, except as perception, you can eliminate and control physical pain.

The last step to enlightenment and unlimited happiness and joy is to have complete control of your emotions.

Imagine that in a while from now you will be able to choose what emotions you want and those that you don't want, and you will be able to switch off anger, jealousy, hatred, sadness, grief, fear and any other emotion that you deem detrimental.

Many decisions that we make, that then become a habit, behaviour or belief, are made whilst in an emotional state, be it positive or negative.

Either way, when we are emotional, we are not

functioning at an optimal level. The best emotional state in which to make clear decisions is neutral. Neutral or zero emotion may be a concept that is hard to grasp, as it is natural to believe that we are always feeling something emotionally.

This is true until you have the learned ability to access a neutral emotional level at will, instantly in any given situation.

This chapter and the audio that accompanies this chapter will train your mind to do this.

When I first broached the idea that this was possible for us as humans to do, many suggested that being able to switch off or increase our emotions at will, made us somehow more robotic or machine like, somehow less human.

Having given this some thought, and having for some time now, been able to access a neutral emotional state for myself at will, I venture to suggest that having this ability makes us a more advanced human being. I will go even further and venture to suggest that it is in fact the next evolution of mankind.

It is quite natural to accept that our emotions and thoughts, just are, and there is nothing we can do about it.

Whether we want to admit it or not, we often indulge ourselves in negative emotions as if it were our right. 'I have a right to be angry'. 'I have a right to be upset'. 'I have a right to feel hurt'.

The left hemisphere of the brain then quite literally makes stuff up to justify our consequent behaviour, even though at an 'essence' level we know it is wrong, detrimental or even ridiculous.

On and on it goes, and we get swallowed up in our own ridiculousness.

This book is not about excuses, judgement, justification or accusations, we all have to look within to answer those questions and recognise that if we are not absolutely honest with ourself, the left hemisphere of the brain will just make stuff up to make you feel better about yourself.

Let us waste no more time talking about this, the next chapter will explain how you can do this for yourself and if you prefer you can listen to the audio that accompanies this chapter. Before you do so though, take the time to prepare yourself for the changes that will happen in your life and relationships once you have complete control of your emotions.

READY?

## Chapter 9
## Total perception management for accessing neutral emotion

This psychological technique will take a while to read and embed unconsciously, and needs to be read completely, without distraction or interruption. So, if you are unable to do that now, please wait until you do have the time and the space to do so. The same applies to the audio session of this technique.
https://freddyjacquin.com/neutralemotion

This technique incorporates The Arrow technique that you learned to eliminate emotional and physical pain.

TPM (Total Perception Management)

As you read these words, do your utmost to imagine what I am describing, in whatever way comes to mind.

Now sit as comfortably as you can and as you read these words let your imagination run.

Take a deep breath in and as you exhale start to feel your body relaxing, more and more with each breath.

Imagine as you do this that you are beginning to drift up out of your body and leaving your body in the chair.

You may even be able to see yourself sitting in the chair reading these words as you drift higher and further away from your body.

Imagine that you are drifting higher and higher, like a helium balloon that a young child has let go of in the park, drifting higher and higher, further and further away from your body in that chair.

Imagine now that you have drifted so high that you can look down and see the planet Earth below you, you can see that beautiful blue planet in your mind's eye.

You can see the whites of the mountain tops, the white of the clouds, the green of the forest and the blue of the ocean.

Notice as you watch that beautiful planet from so far away, how your perspective changes.

You can think about the 7 billion people living on that planet of which you are one, notice as you think about that how things that had seemed overwhelming, no longer have any power over you, things that had seemed difficult, even impossible, no longer have any power over you.

Now in your mind's eye picture a target, like an archery target way down below you, between you and that beautiful blue planet, a massive target, you can see the coloured bands and you can see the very centre of that target.

In the centre of the target is every ounce of emotion that you were experiencing.

In a moment you will read a specific word, an instruction, and as you read that word you will feel yourself propelled through space in your mind, like an arrow.

You will feel yourself fly right through the centre of the target in a millisecond and out the other side into a space of bliss, but I want you to be brave because as you fly through the centre of the target you will experience those emotions even more intensely for a split second, but be brave, as you exit the target you will experience zero emotions, a neutral emotional state.
So, get ready for the word.

*NOW*

And now you are through the target and out the other side just floating in a space of zero emotion.

Now imagine drifting across the other side of your room so that you can see yourself sitting in that chair reading.

You can see the clothes that you are wearing and notice as you watch yourself reading from the other side of the room how every ounce of emotion has gone from your mind and your body. You cannot feel it, you cannot experience it.

The harder you try and remember what emotion felt like, the further from you mind it goes.

Now as you read this, your mind will allow you to drift back over to your body in that chair and drop down and reintegrate back into your body, unable to feel any emotion.

Now as you experience zero emotion, click you fingers once.

Take a breath and as you continue to experience zero emotions, click your fingers again; and from this moment on whenever you want to return to neutral emotion, you click your fingers once and you will instantly return to neutral.

Take a couple of deep breaths now and you will return to your normal emotional state.

You can return to this chapter or audio as often as you need to for you to master this technique.

Remember that being able to access a neutral emotional state enables us to make the right decisions, take the right actions to create the right outcome.

Where attention goes, energy flows. Always bring your attention back to, and focus on, the life you want to create, and your mind and body will create the right energetic state to accomplish it.

Just for a moment, in your mind's eye go out into a future time when you are living the life you truly want.

Notice the way that you move and breathe. Step into your body in that future and feel what it feels like to have achieved it. See what you will see, hear what you will hear, feel what you will feel, that feeling of achievement, the confidence and the self-esteem.

Look back to now and notice all the things that you did along the way, that lead to achieving that wonderful life.

Because now that you know how you will feel when you achieve that life and you know how to get there, there is not a force on this planet that will keep you from achieving your dream life.

This book promised you unlimited happiness and this next chapter will teach you how to use TPM to increase a positive emotional state, joy, love, pleasure, passion, fun and of course happiness.

I will explain how you can do this for yourself and if you prefer you can listen to the audio that accompanies this chapter.

Before you do so though take the time to prepare yourself for the changes that will happen in your life and relationships once you have complete control of your emotions.

## Chapter 10
## TPM to increase a positive emotional state

As with the previous technique, this psychological technique will take a while to read and embed unconsciously, and needs to be read completely, without distraction or interruption.

So, if you are unable to do that now, please wait until you do have the time and the space to do so. The same applies to the audio session of this technique. https://freddyjacquin.com/positiveemotion

This technique incorporates The Arrow technique that you learned to eliminate emotional and physical pain and return to neutral emotional state.

TPM (Total Perception Management)

As you read these words, do your utmost to imagine what I am describing, in whatever way comes to mind.

Now sit as comfortably as you can and as you read these words let your imagination run.

Take a deep breath in and as you exhale start to feel

your body relaxing, more and more with each breath.

Imagine as you do this that you are beginning to drift up out of your body and leaving your body in the chair.

You may even be able to see yourself sitting in the chair reading these words as you drift higher and further away from your body.

Imagine that you are drifting higher and higher, like a helium balloon that a young child has let go of in the park, drifting higher and higher, further and further away from your body in that chair.

Imagine now that you have drifted so high that you can look down and see the planet Earth below you, you can see that beautiful blue planet in your mind's eye.

You can see the whites of the mountain tops, the white of the clouds, the green of the forest and the blue of the ocean.

Notice as you watch that beautiful planet from so far away, how your perspective changes.

You can think about the 7 billion people living on

that planet of which you are one, notice as you think about that how things that had seemed overwhelming, no longer have any power over you, things that had seemed difficult even impossible, no longer have any power over you.

Now in your mind's eye picture a target, like an archery target, way down below you between you and that beautiful blue planet, a massive target, you can see the coloured bands and you can see the very centre of that target.

In the centre of the target is every incredible positive emotion that you have ever experienced, love, joy, happiness, pleasure, passion and freedom.

In a moment you will read a specific word, an instruction, and as you read that word you will feel yourself propelled through space in your mind, like an arrow. You will feel yourself fly right through the centre of the target in a millisecond and out the other side into a space of bliss.

As you fly through the centre of the target, your mind and body will be flooded with the most intense experience of positive emotions, love, joy, pleasure, passion and happiness, more intensely than you have ever experienced before. So, get ready for the word.

*NOW*

And now you are through the target and out the other side just floating in a space of total joy, love, happiness and pleasure.

Think of the people you love, people that love you, and feel that love now, like a burning hot sun in a summer sky. Shrink that feeling down to a burning hot ball of light as big as a golf ball and pull that light and love into the very core of your being, into the very centre of your being.

Feel the force of that love and light flooding your body and your mind, spreading into every cell, every molecule, into the very marrow of your bones. Lighting you up lifting you up now.

Now imagine drifting across the other side of your room so that you can see yourself sitting in that chair reading. You can see the clothes that you are wearing and notice, as you watch yourself reading from the other side of the room, how your mind and body is flooded with the most intense experience of positive emotions, love, joy, pleasure, passion and happiness, more intensely than you have ever experienced before.

Now as you read this, your mind will allow you to drift back over to your body in that chair and drop down and reintegrate back into your body, with the most intense experience of positive emotions, love, joy, pleasure, passion and happiness, more intensely than you have ever experienced before.

Now as you continue to experience these wonderful emotions, click you fingers twice, rapidly and notice as you do that that the feelings increase.

Take a breath in and as you continue to experience these incredible wonderful emotions click your fingers again twice rapidly, and from this moment on whenever you want to increase a positive emotion, you click your fingers twice and you will instantly increase the pleasure and joy you are feeling.

Take a couple of deep breaths now and you will return to your normal emotional state.

You can return to this chapter or audio as often as you need to for you to master this technique.

## Chapter 11

### Need, want and desire

### Manifesting your dreams:

The majority, of us at times in our life want something, we may desire to have something. A certain car, a certain kind of relationship, physique, amount of money, house etc. More often, than not we never actualise these wants and desires.

You will by now, if you have followed the instructions in this book and used the audio sessions, realise how much more you are, and how much more you can achieve that you previously believed.

The last and final step in achieving enlightenment and unlimited happiness is to manifest your dreams, goals, and desires.

These next few pages will show you how.

Firstly though, we must understand the difference between, 'wanting', 'desiring' and 'needing'.

As I stated earlier in this book, for a goal to be achieved, a few things must be in place. You must have an absolute and exciting goal, and it has to be time bound.

We can as we often do, want something, and sometimes wanting something leads to us acquiring it.

We can desire something or someone and sometimes we achieve that goal.

If you place a metal paper clip close enough to a magnet, the magnetic energy created will move that clip and even pull the clip onto the magnet. The magnetic force or energy that creates that pull or attraction, although incredibly powerful, cannot be seen.

The planet earth has an incredible magnetic force, this force is all around us and within us. All magnetic material is affected by this force.

As human beings we also have a magnetic force or energy, and as with all magnetic force fields this force cannot be seen, only felt. There are many terms given to this magnetic energy and many ways of creating it.

The most, commonly known, albeit not often identified as such, are confidence and charisma.

This same magnetic force field can be utilised to achieve our life goals. These magnetic forces can be described as our, wants, desire and needs, and as with all magnets the strength of each magnet varies.

The weakest is, 'Wanting'. We all want things, but this rarely leads to having that thing, person, or object.

The next in scale of magnetic pull is, 'desire'. We often desire something or someone, yet again though, this rarely leads to those desires being fulfilled.

The most powerful force in a human is, 'need'. If you truly need something to thrive or exist every part of your being will strive to achieve it.

This innate powerful force exists in all animals. If an animal needs water, it will instinctively know where to find it. This, same ability exists in us all, and explains how water divining works for humans.

This is just one clear example of these unseen forces within us.

Knowing the power of, 'need' we can utilise this force to achieve what we want and desire.

So how do we do this?

As an example, let us take one of the most common desires, the desire to lose weight. The weight loss industry is worth billions because most people, yoyo diet and never maintain their ideal weight. The reasons for this are many but the main reason is that they have not identified the 'need'.

If you identify why you need to lose weight and keep the weight off, then identify why you want to do it and make this clear to your mind so that it becomes your hearts, desire, both conscious and unconscious aspects of your mind and both hemispheres of your brain will align, and every aspect of your being will create the magnetic energy that will attract that outcome.

This then is how you manifest your dreams:

1. Let go of any limiting beliefs and think about what you truly want. Use all your senses, you can do this now.

    1a) Imagine a time in the future where you have achieved this goal.

    1b)) Step into the body of that future you and physically feel what you will feel when you have achieved it

1c) See what you will see when you have achieved it.

1d) Hear what you will hear.

1e) Make this visualisation and experience so compelling that it becomes your hearts, desire.

2. Identify, or if needs be, create the need for what you want.
   2a) You need this because…………………………
   your happiness, your self-esteem, your well-being, and your life in this moment and in your future depends on you achieving this.

3. Now make this your hearts, desire and hold that feeling.

   If you have taken the time out to do this, thoroughly you will have already begun to generate the magnetic force that will draw into your life everything that is necessary for you to achieve your desire outcome.

Let go of any perceived limitations or doubts, remember they were never originally yours and were only ever someone else's opinion.

Remember, times waits for no man, do it now!

## Chapter 12
## Enlightenment and unlimited happiness:
## Putting it all together

I used the analogy at the beginning of this book, that creating your dream life was like building your dream house.

Providing that you have actively participated in the techniques described in this book or have listened to the audios that accompany this book, you will have cleared the building plot of all the rubbish, blocks, fears, limiting beliefs, negative thoughts and doubts.

You will have put in deep foundations, of self-belief, self-esteem and self-worth by recognising that you are not your thoughts or physical being, that the essence of who you are is infinite and endless, you are the universe within a body.

You will have started to build the structure of your dream house by eliminating any useless, unnecessary emotional or physical pain or discomfort.

The house now stands on firm foundations of love, joy and happiness. You have control of the elements by having complete control of your emotional state.

You can now choose the interior decorations and furniture, the things that bring you joy, happiness, love and kindness.

You no longer need to wait to be happy, you are already happy, and now you have the ability, to ramp up and increase any positive emotion including, but not limited to, happiness, joy and love.

Knowing that you can choose exactly which emotions you want to eliminate or increase, you can live your life, apart from and a part of the matrix that we call life, on your own terms.

To love fearlessly and to allow yourself to be loved without conditions, constraints or limits.

What is enlightenment if not the knowledge that you are all you need to be right here and right now, to be present in this moment to experience this wonderful human existence to the max.

I wish you a wonderful existence now and forevermore.

From my essence to your essence.
My Best Regards and love, always.

Freddy

Other titles by this author: Available on Amazon.

**'Hypnotherapy'**
Methods, techniques and philosophies of Freddy H Jacquin.

Novels:
**'Messiah'**
'Can one man change the world'?

**'Hypnotised'**

Children's books series:
**'The Mesmers'**


Associated websites

www.freddyjacquin.com
www.jacquinhypnosisacademy.com

My sincere thanks once again to Felicia J Ursarescu, for the beautiful art, used throughout this book.

Printed in Great Britain
by Amazon